Introduction

We all love to knit for the special "little" people in our lives—babies and toddlers. Having their very own "blankie" gives children comfort and security. And doesn't it do our own hearts good to knit such wonderful gifts!

These six easy projects are designed with basic knit and purl stitches and borders that are knitted in as you go along. When you're done, you're done!

Design Directory

Raspberry Rib Blankie
Page 2

Candy Stripes Blankie
Page 4

Mint Melody Blankie
Page 6

Sunny Weave Blankie
Page 8

Tailored Blues Blankie
Page 10

Summer Meadow Blankie
Page 12

American School of Needlework • Berne, Indiana 46711 • DRGnetwork.com

Easy Timeless Blankies • 1

Raspberry Rib Blankie

Skill Level
 EASY

Sizes
Baby (Toddler) Instructions are given for smaller size, with larger size in parentheses. When only 1 number is given, it applies to both sizes.

Finished Measurements
Approximately 30 x 40 (36 x 44) inches

Materials
Bernat Baby Coordinates lightweight yarn (431 yds/160g per skein): 2 (3) skeins sweet pink #09412
Size 7 (4.5mm) 32-inch circular needle or size needed to obtain gauge
Tapestry needle
Stitch markers

Gauge
Approximately 17 sts = 4 inches/10cm in pat st
To save time, take time to check gauge.

Pattern Stitch
Barley Sugar Rib (multiple of 6 sts)
Row 1 (RS): *K3, p3; rep from * across.
Rows 2 and 3: Rep Row 1.
Row 4: *P1, k3, p2; rep from * across.
Row 5: Knit the knit sts and purl the purl sts.
Row 6: Rep Row 4.
Row 7: *K1, p3, k2; rep from * across.
Row 8: Rep Row 5.
Row 9: Rep Row 7.
Rows 10, 11 and 12: *P3, k3; rep from * across.
Row 13: *P2, k3, p1; rep from * across.
Row 14: Rep Row 5.
Row 15: Rep Row 13.
Row 16: *K2, p3, k1; rep from * across.
Row 17: Rep Row 5.
Row 18: Rep Row 16.
Rep Rows 1-18 for pat.

Pattern Notes
Circular needle is used to accommodate large number of sts. Do not join, work back and forth in rows.
Since this pat is reversible it is helpful to mark Row 1 as RS row.

Instructions

Cast on 128 (154) sts.
Knit 12 (20) rows.
K7 (11), place marker, work Row 1 of Barley Sugar Rib pat over next 114 (132) sts, place marker, k7 (11).
Continue in pat as established working first and last 7 (11) sts in garter st and sts between markers in Barley Sugar Rib pat until piece measures approximately 38¾ (41¾) inches from beg.
Knit 12 (20) rows.
Bind off.
Weave in ends and block to measurements. ●

Candy Stripes Blankie

Skill Level
■■□□ EASY

Sizes
Baby (Toddler) Instructions are given for smaller size, with larger size in parentheses. When only 1 number is given, it applies to both sizes.

Finished Measurements
Approximately 30 x 40 (36 x 44) inches

Materials
- Bernat Cottontots medium weight cotton yarn (150 yds/85g per skein): 7 (9) skeins sweet dreams #91231
- Size 7 (4.5mm) 32-inch circular needle or size needed to obtain gauge
- Tapestry needle
- Stitch markers

Gauge
Approximately 18 sts = 4 inches/10cm in pat
To save time, take time to check gauge.

Pattern Stitches
A. Modified Farrow Rib (multiple of 4 sts)
Row 1: *K3, p1; rep from * across.
Rep Row 1 for pat.

B. Moss St (multiple of 2 sts)
Row 1 (RS): *K1, p1; rep from * across.
Row 2: *P1, k1; rep from * across.
Rep Rows 1 and 2 for pat.

Pattern Note
Circular needle is used to accommodate large number of sts. Do not join, work back and forth in rows.

Instructions
Cast on 136 (164) sts.
Work [Rows 1 and 2 of Moss St pat] 5 (7) times.
Work 6 (10) sts Moss St Pat as established, place marker, work Modified Farrow Rib pat over next 124 (144) sts, place marker, work 6 (10) sts in Moss St pat as established.
Continue in pats as established, working first and last 6 (10) sts in Moss St pat and sts between markers in Modified Farrow Rib pat until piece measures approximately 38½ (42) inches from beg.
Work in 10 (14) rows in Moss St pat.
Bind off.
Weave in ends and block to measurements. ●

Mint Melody Blankie

Skill Level
■■□□ EASY

Sizes
Baby (Toddler) Instructions are given for smaller size, with larger size in parentheses. When only 1 number is given it applies to both sizes.

Finished Measurements
Approximately 30 x 40 (36 x 44) inches

Materials
Bernat Cottontots medium weight cotton yarn (171 yds/100g per skein): 5 (7) skeins sweet green #90230
Size 7 (4.5mm) 32-inch circular needle or size needed to obtain gauge
Tapestry needle
Stitch markers

Gauge
Approximately 18 sts = 4 inches/10cm in pat st
To save time, take time to check gauge.

Pattern Stitch
Dotted Line (multiple of 2)
Row 1 (RS): Knit.
Row 2: Purl.
Rows 3 and 4: Rep Rows 1 and 2.
Row 5: *K1, p1; rep from * across.
Row 6: Rep Row 2.
Rep Rows 1–6 for pat.

Pattern Note
Circular needle is used to accommodate large number of sts. Do not join, work back and forth in rows.

Instructions
Cast on 136 (162) sts.
Knit 12 (20) rows.
K7 (11), place marker, work Row 1 of Dotted Line pat over next 122 (140) sts, place marker, k7 (11).
Continue in pat as established, working first and last 7 (11) sts in garter st and sts between markers in pat st until piece measures approximately 38½ (41½) inches from beg, ending by working a Row 3 of Dotted Line pat.
Knit 12 (20) rows.
Bind off.
Weave in ends and block to measurements. ●

Sunny Weave Blankie

Skill Level
■■□□ EASY

Sizes
Baby (Toddler) Instructions are given for smaller size, with larger size in parentheses. When only 1 number is given, it applies to both sizes.

Finished Measurements
Approximately 30 x 40 (36 x 44) inches

Materials
Bernat Baby Bouclé bulky weight yarn (180 yds/100g per skein): 4 (5) skeins soft lemon #00104
Size 8 (5.0mm) 32-inch circular needle or size needed to obtain gauge
Tapestry needle
Stitch markers

Gauge
Approximately 15 sts = 4 inches/10cm in pat st
To save time, take time to check gauge.

Pattern Stitch
Nubby Basket Weave (multiple of 12 sts)
Row 1 (RS): Knit.
Row 2: Purl.
Rows 3–6: *K6, p6; rep from * across.
Row 7: Purl.
Row 8: Knit.
Rows 9–12: *K6, p6; rep from * across.
Row 13: Knit.
Row 14: Purl.
Rows 15–18: *P6, k6; rep from * across.
Row 19: Purl.
Row 20: Knit.
Rows 21–24: *P6, k6; rep from * across.
Rep Rows 1–24 for pat.

Pattern Notes
Circular needle is used to accommodate large number of sts. Do not join, work back and forth in rows.
Since this pat is reversible, it is helpful to mark Row 1 as the RS row.

Instructions
Cast on 112 (134) sts.
Knit 13 (23) rows.
K8 (13), place marker, work Row 1 of Nubby Basket Weave pat over next 96 (108) sts, place marker, k8 (13).
Continue in pats as established, working first and last 8 (13) sts in garter st and sts between markers in Nubby Basket Weave pat until piece measures approximately 38 (40½) inches from beg, ending by working a Row 12 or Row 24 of pat.
Knit 13 (23) rows.
Bind off.
Weave in end and block to measurements. ●

Tailored Blues Blankie

Skill Level
■■□□ EASY

Sizes
Baby (Toddler) Instructions are given for smaller size, with larger size in parentheses. When only 1 number is given it applies to both sizes.

Finished Measurements
Approximately 30 x 40 (36 x 44) inches

Materials
Lion Brand Babysoft lightweight yarn (459 yds/141g per skein): 3 (4) skeins pastel blue #106
Size 6 (4.0mm) 32-inch circular needle or size needed to obtain gauge
Tapestry needle
Stitch markers

Gauge
Approximately 20.5 sts = 4 inches/10cm in pat st
To save time, take time to check gauge.

Pattern Stitches
A. Stripe (multiple of 16 sts + 10)
Row 1 (RS): K10, *[p1, k1] 3 times, K10; rep from * across.
Row 2: *P10, [k1, p1] 3 times; rep from * to last 10 sts, p10.
Rep Rows 1 and 2 for pat.

B. Moss Stitch (even number of sts)
Row 1 (RS): *K1, p1; rep from * across.
Row 2 (WS): *P1, k1; rep from * across.
Rep Rows 1 and 2 for pat.

C. Moss Stitch (odd number of sts)
Row 1: Knit the purl sts and purl the knit sts across.
Rep Row 1 for pat.

Pattern Note
Circular needle is used to accommodate large number of sts. Do not join, work back and forth in rows.

Instructions
Cast on 152 (184) sts.
Work in Moss St pat for 12 (24) rows.
Work 7 (15) sts in Moss St pat as established, place marker, work Row 1 of Stripe pat over next 138 (154) sts, work rem 7 (15) sts in Moss St pat as established.
Continue in pats as established, working first and last 7 (15) sts in Moss St pat and sts between markers in Stripe pat until piece measures approximately 38¾ (41½) inches from beg.
Work in Moss St pat for 12 (24) rows.
Bind off.
Weave in ends and block to measurements. ●

Summer Meadow Blankie

Skill Level
■■□□ EASY

Sizes
Baby (Toddler) Instructions are given for smaller size, with larger size in parentheses. When only 1 number is given, it applies to both sizes.

Finished Measurements
Approximately 30 x 40 (36 x 44) inches

Materials
- Lion Brand Homespun bulky weight yarn (185 yds/170g per skein): 3 (4) skeins Florida Keys green #369
- Size 9 (5.5mm) 32-inch circular needle or size needed to obtain gauge
- Tapestry needle
- Stitch markers

Gauge
Approximately 12 sts = 4 inches/10cm in pat
To save time, take time to check gauge.

Pattern Stitches
A. Ridged Squares (multiple of 5 sts + 4)
Row 1 (RS): *K4, p1; rep from * across to last 4 sts, k4.
Row 2: *P4, k1; rep from * across to last 4 sts, p4.
Rows 3 and 4: Rep Rows 1 and 2.
Row 5: Rep Row 1.
Row 6: Knit.
Rep Rows 1–6 for pat.

B. Moss Stitch (even number of sts)
Row 1 (RS): *K1, p1; rep from * across.
Row 2: *P1, k1; rep from * across.
Rep Rows 1 and 2 for pat.

C. Moss Stitch (odd number of sts)
Row 1: Purl the knit sts and knit the purl sts.
Rep Row 1 for pat.

Pattern Note
Circular needle is used to accommodate large number of sts. Do not join, work back and forth in rows.

Instructions
Cast on 90 (106) sts.
Work in Moss St pat for 4 (10) rows.
Work 3 (6) sts in Moss St pat as established, place marker, work Row 1 of Ridged Squares pat over next 84 (94) sts, place marker, work 3 (6) sts in Moss St pat as established.
Continue in pats as established, working first and last 3 (6) sts in Moss St pat and sts between markers in Ridged Squares pat until piece measures approximately 39 (42) inches, ending with Row 4 of Ridged Squares pat.
Work in Moss St pat for 4 (10) rows.
Bind off.
Weave in ends and block if necessary. ●

General Information

Knit Abbreviations & Symbols

approx . . . . . approximately
beg . . . . . begin/beginning
CC . . . . . contrasting color
ch . . . . . chain stitch
cm . . . . . centimeter(s)
cn . . . . . cable needle
dec . . . . decrease/decreases/decreasing
dpn(s) . double-pointed needle(s)
g . . . . . gram
inc . increase/increases/increasing
k . . . . . knit
k2tog . . knit 2 stitches together
LH . . . . . left hand
lp(s) . . . . . loop(s)
m . . . . . meter(s)
M1 . . . . . make one stitch
MC . . . . . main color
mm . . . . . millimeter(s)
oz . . . . . ounce(s)
p . . . . . purl
pat(s) . . . . . pattern(s)
p2tog . . purl 2 stitches together
psso . . . pass slipped stitch over
p2sso . pass 2 slipped stitches over
rem . . . . . remain/remaining
rep . . . . . repeat(s)
rev St st . reverse stockinette stitch
RH . . . . . right hand
rnd(s) . . . . . rounds
RS . . . . . right side
skp . . slip, knit, pass stitch over—one stitch decreased
sk2p . . . slip 1, knit 2 together, pass slip stitch over, then knit 2 together—2 stitches have been decreased
sl . . . . . slip
sl 1k . . . . . slip 1 knitwise
sl 1p . . . . . slip 1 purlwise
sl st . . . . . slip stitch(es)
ssk . . slip, slip, knit these 2 stitches together—a decrease
st(s) . . . . . stitch(es)
St st . . . . . stockinette stitch/stocking stitch
tbl . . . . . through back loop(s)
tog . . . . . together
WS . . . . . wrong side
wyib . . . . . with yarn in back
wyif . . . . . with yarn in front
yd(s) . . . . . yard(s)
yfwd . . . . . yarn forward
yo(s) . . . . . yarn over(s)

[ ] work instructions within brackets as many times as directed
( ) work instructions within parentheses in the place directed
** repeat instructions following the asterisks as directed
* repeat instructions following the single asterisk as directed
" inch(es)

How to Check Gauge

A correct stitch gauge is very important. Please take the time to work a stitch gauge swatch about 4 x 4 inches. Measure the swatch. If the number of stitches and rows are fewer than indicated under "Gauge" in the pattern, your needles are too large. Try another swatch with smaller-size needles. If the number of stitches and rows are more than indicated under "Gauge" in the pattern, your needles are too small. Try another swatch with larger-size needles.

Inches Into Millimeters & Centimeters

All measurements are rounded off slightly.

inches	mm	cm	inches	cm	inches	cm	inches	cm
⅛	3	0.3	5	12.5	21	53.5	38	96.5
¼	6	0.6	5½	14	22	56.0	39	99.0
⅜	10	1.0	6	15.0	23	58.5	40	101.5
½	13	1.3	7	18.0	24	61.0	41	104.0
⅝	15	1.5	8	20.5	25	63.5	42	106.5
¾	20	2.0	9	23.0	26	66.0	43	109.0
⅞	22	2.2	10	25.5	27	68.5	44	112.0
1	25	2.5	11	28.0	28	71.0	45	114.5
1¼	32	3.8	12	30.5	29	73.5	46	117.0
1½	38	3.8	13	33.0	30	76.0	47	119.5
1¾	45	4.5	14	35.5	31	79.0	48	122.0
2	50	5.0	15	38.0	32	81.5	49	124.5
2½	65	6.5	16	40.5	33	84.0	50	127.0
3	75	7.5	17	43.0	34	86.5		
3½	90	9.0	18	46.0	35	89.0		
4	100	10.0	19	48.5	36	91.5		
4½	115	11.5	20	51.0	37	94.0		

Knitting Needle Conversion Chart

U.S.	1	2	3	4	5	6	7	8	9	10	10½	11	13	15	17	19	35	50
Continental-mm	2.25	2.75	3.25	3.5	3.75	4	4.5	5	5.5	6	6.5	8	9	10	12.75	15	19	25

Skill Levels

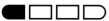
BEGINNER
Beginner projects for first-time knitters using basic stitches. Minimal shaping.

EASY
Easy projects using basic stitches, repetitive stitch patterns, simple color changes and simple shaping and finishing.

INTERMEDIATE
Intermediate projects with a variety of stitches, mid-level shaping and finishing.

EXPERIENCED
Experienced projects using advanced techniques and stitches, detailed shaping and refined finishing.

Standard Yarn Weight System
Categories of yarn, gauge ranges, and recommended needle sizes

Yarn Weight Symbol & Category Names	1 SUPER FINE	2 FINE	3 LIGHT	4 MEDIUM	5 BULKY	6 SUPER BULKY
Type of Yarns in Category	Sock, Fingering, Baby	Sport, Baby	DK, Light Worsted	Worsted, Afghan, Aran	Chunky, Craft, Rug	Bulky, Roving
Knit Gauge Range* in Stockinette Stitch to 4 inches	27–32 sts	23–26 sts	21–24 sts	16–20 sts	12–15 sts	6–11 sts
Recommended Needle in Metric Size Range	2.25–3.25mm	3.25–3.75mm	3.75–4.5mm	4.5–5.5mm	5.5–8mm	8mm and larger
Recommended Needle U.S. Size Range	1 to 3	3 to 5	5 to 7	7 to 9	9 to 11	11 and larger

* **GUIDELINES ONLY:** The above reflect the most commonly used gauges and needle sizes for specific yarn categories.

Copyright © 2007 DRG, 306 East Parr Road, Berne, IN 46711. All rights reserved.
This publication may not be reproduced in part or in whole without written permission from the publisher.

TOLL-FREE ORDER LINE or to request a free catalog (800) 582-6643
Customer Service (800) 282-6643, **Fax** (800) 882-6643
Visit DRGnetwork.com.

We have made every effort to ensure the accuracy and completeness of these instructions.
We cannot, however, be responsible for human error, typographical mistakes or variations in individual work.

ISBN: 978-1-59012-205-1   All rights reserved.   Printed in USA   1 2 3 4 5 6 7 8 9